ideals
FRIENDSHIP

Vol. 47, No. 6

Publisher, Patricia A. Pingry
Associate Editor, Nancy Skarmeas
Photography and Permissions Editor,
  Kathleen Gilbert
Art Director, Patrick McRae
Editorial Assistant, Fran Morley
Contributing Editor, Bonnie Aeschliman

ISBN 0-8249-1085-0

IDEALS—Vol. 47, No. 6 September MCMXC IDEALS
(ISSN 0019-137X) is published eight times a year: Febru-
ary, March, May, June, August, September, November,
December by IDEALS PUBLISHING CORPORATION,
Nelson Place at Elm Hill Pike, Nashville, Tenn. 37214.
Second-class postage paid at Nashville, Tennessee, and
additional mailing offices. Copyright © MCMXC by IDE-
ALS PUBLISHING CORPORATION. POSTMASTER:
Send address changes to Ideals, Post Office Box 148000,
Nashville, Tenn. 37214-8000. All rights reserved. Title
IDEALS registered U.S. Patent Office.

SINGLE ISSUE—$4.95
ONE-YEAR SUBSCRIPTION—eight consecutive issues as
published—$19.95
TWO-YEAR SUBSCRIPTION—sixteen consecutive issues
as published—$35.95
Outside U.S.A., add $6.00 per subscription year for postage
and handling.

ACKNOWLEDGMENTS

LITTLE BOY DRESSING from *LIVING THE YEARS* by
Edgar A. Guest. Copyright 1949 by The Reilly & Lee Co.
Used by permission of the Estate; IF I COULD MAKE A
FRIEND from *COME ON HOME* by Douglas Malloch,
copyright 1923. Used by permission of the Estate;
HAPPY GIRLS from *EARTHBOUND NO LONGER* by
Caroline Eyring Miner, copyright 1961. Used by permission; MY FIRESIDE FRIEND from *SMILE ALONG THE
WAY* by Virginia Katherine Oliver, copyright 1946. Used
by permission of the Estate; MY THANKS FOR OTHERS
from *AN OLD CRACKED CUP* by Margaret Rorke. Copy-
right © 1980 by Northwood Institute Press. Used by permission of the author. Our sincere thanks to the following
whose addresses we were unable to locate: Linnea Holmberg Bodman for OLD FRIENDS; Betty Collier for
RETURN OF AUTUMN; Georgia Moore Eberling for MY
HEART IS KNOWING; Maxine Hartley for THE FAMILY
WITHIN; Roy Z. Kemp for HOSPITALITY; Eunice Mackin-
son for INTERIOR DECORATING; Blythe Gwyn Sears for
AUTUMN MEMORIES; Betty W. Stoffel for TO A SHUT-
IN; May Smith White for PRAYER FOR A FRIEND.

Four-color separations by Rayson Films, Inc., Waukesha,
Wisconsin

Printing by Ringier-America, Brookfield, Wisconsin

The paper used in this publication meets the minimum
requirements of American National Standard for Information Sciences—Permanence of Paper for Printed
Library Materials, ANSI Z39.48-1984.

Cover Photo
Dietrich Stock Photos, Inc.

If I Could
Make a Friend

Douglas Malloch

If I could make a friend today
I would not ask for greater store;
If just one soul would come and say,
"We shall be comrades evermore,"
I would not need to count my gold
Tonight when all my labors end—
My heart a greater wealth would hold
If I could say, "I made a friend."

If I could have a friend tonight
I did not have at this day's dawn
One hand that held my fingers tight,
One breast that I could lean upon,
I would not need to calculate
How much my profit, how much my trade,
My gain today to estimate,
If I could say, "A friend I made."

If I today a friend could find
Amid the labor and the stress,
Some toiling brother, kindred mind,
Some hand to clasp in tenderness,
It would not matter what reward
The hours had brought me on the way,
If I could say, "I thank Thee, Lord—
I know I made a friend today."

Photo Opposite
Morning Glories
Thomas/H. Armstrong Roberts, Inc.

Farewell to Summer

Elisabeth Weaver Winstead

A message stirs in the dry, crisp air
That sweeps each sight and sound,
The crickets croon a steady tune
As rustling leaves drift down.

Now all the singing swallows
From woods and meadows go,
In valleys and shaded hollows
Damp, billowing breezes blow.

The blossoms of gleaming asters
Show yellow, bronze, and red,
Where yesterday grew a profusion
Of crimson dahlias instead.

We bid goodbye to summer,
Fresh fragrance of new-mown hay;
I know that soon treasured summer
Will silently tiptoe away.

Farewell to green-slippered summer,
Rare storehouse of life and birth,
Shining splendors of the countryside,
The warm rich rhapsody of earth.

Northeast Harbor, Maine
Fred Sieb Photographer

The Apples Are Ripe

Cindy Guentherman

The wind knows a secret;
    it calls through the trees
And rattles the branches
    like brittle old keys.
For locked in protection
    of leaves and brown limbs
Are treasures more precious
    than gold, oil, or gems.
The apples are ripe!
    oh, I'll yell it again—
The apples are ready!
    and you'll know it when
You reach up and pluck one
    and take that first bite
Of sweet juicy crispness;
    you'll yell with delight—
The apples are ripe!
    green, yellow, and red,

So let's drag the baskets
    from out of the shed.
Climb the old ladder
    and isn't it grand
To feel how each fruit
    lies cupped in your hand.
Shine them up gently
    and see each one glow
In dappled fall sunlight
    and always you know
That the first bite will sound
    like a crackle of fire.
Oh, the apples are ripe,
    and I never tire
Of gazing at trees
    in those old orchards where
I can breathe the sweet smells
    of ripe-apple air.

Photo Opposite
Cider Press
Dianne Dietrich Leis Photo

Photo Overleaf
Country Road
East Orange, Vermont
Fred M. Dole Productions

All the Lovely Things Must Go

Thomas Curtis Clark

All the lovely things must go—
Hyacinths and daffodils,
Cherry blossoms white as snow,
Violets on greening hills;

Roses born of sunny June,
Hollyhock and golden-glow:
Summer passes all too soon,
All the lovely things must go.

They will vanish, so today
I must live and laugh and sing,
Garner beauty by the way,
Cherishing each perfect thing.

Then when winter brings the cold
And the cerements of snow,
I shall have some dreams to hold,
Though the lovely things must go.

Photo Opposite
Country Store
South Woodstock, Vermor
Fred M. Dole Productions

FRIENDSHIP'S DOOR

Carice Williams

The keys that open friendship's door
Are in your hands and mine.
There's a key called understanding
Fashioned from a rare design;
For this quiet understanding
That is passed from friend to friend
Is what makes a pleasant friendship
Keep blooming with no end.

There's another key most precious
That can open friendship's door;
It's called love and we must use it
Each day, more and more
For if we give ourselves all freely
Ever seeking for the best—
Being blind to faults of others—
Then true friendship's been expressed.

My Fireside Friend

Virginia Katherine Oliver

In the quiet twilight hour
My fireside friend and I
Sit and watch the dying embers
And watch the night draw nigh.

There is such a peaceful feeling
Descending over all
In that sacred, solemn stillness
When night begins to fall.

Frequently the fading firelight
Casts shadows across the floor,
And I can see my fireside friend
There close beside the door.

And I know my friend is thinking,
Just much the same as I,
How we love this hour together
When night is drawing nigh.

Jessie Walker, Photographer

Prayer for a Friend

May Smith White

This is my prayer
for you each day:

That paths grow bright
along your way;

That love will be
your steadfast guide—

God walking always
by your side.

Deana Deck

Window Boxes

In Mediterranean villages you see them at every window, overflowing with brilliant color. In cities throughout Europe they perch on windowsills and balconies, high above cobbled streets, blooms cascading down the sides of ancient buildings. Throughout the British Isles you'll see them crowded with nasturtiums and miniature dahlias. In our country, however, if you see them at all they are usually empty and abandoned, except for the occasional weed forlornly peeking out of hard-packed, barren soil.

They are window boxes, and they used to be a common sight beneath the windows of American homes, but since the coming of central heating and cooling systems, hermetically sealed windows and the thermostat, window boxes have just about gone the way of dinosaurs.

People used to open their windows more often to cool and ventilate their homes, and a box of fragrant blooms on the windowsill bridged the gap between the indoor world and the outdoor one, adding color and fragrance to living spaces. From the open window, seeds could be planted, young plants tended and watered, and blooms picked to be placed on the breakfast table.

Today we have patios and decks that bring the outdoors inside, but they lack the charm and gaiety of a window box. Still, most garden supply companies do offer window boxes, usually referred to as planters. They're marketed more for use as patio or porch containers, but are easily installed under a handy window.

Window boxes are also easy to construct from raw materials. In most garden centers inexpensive booklets are available featuring wood projects to build for the garden. Most include a section on designing and constructing window boxes.

The best materials to use are redwood or cedar, both of which are rot resistant. Redwood, which is fairly expensive, is preferable because it does not require painting. Neither does cedar, if you like the natural gray to which it weathers. If you're planning to paint the boxes to match shutters or other trim, then build them out of low-cost, pressure-treated pine. It's always a good idea to paint the inside of the boxes with a polyurethane sealer to prolong the life of the wood, which will be kept constantly moist if you take good care of your plants. And be sure to provide ample drainage by drilling holes in the bottoms of the boxes.

Once you have your box, there are a variety of options for planting. The simplest way is to place potted flowers right into the window box, pot and all. Just add a bit of gravel to the bottom of the box to facilitate drainage. This set-up makes it convenient to change your flowers from season to season. If you decide to go this route, select plastic pots, as opposed to clay ones. The plastic will retain moisture longer and you won't have to water as frequently as with clay pots.

The beauty of using potted plants in window boxes, of course, is that the contents can be easily changed with the seasons. You can start tulip, daffodil, or hyacinth bulbs indoors in late winter, and with the first warm days of spring, set the pots into window boxes for an instant garden. When the bulbs have finished blooming, the pots can be removed to an out-of-the-way location while the foliage progresses through its unattractive but necessary life cycle of gradual withering and bulb replenishment.

Bulb pots can be replaced with pots of miniature roses, or with geraniums, petunias, marigolds, or other small annuals which will bloom all summer. In fall, replace the fading summer plants with pots of chrysanthemums, dwarf asters, or miniature dahlias; in winter, sprays of holly or pine keep the box attractive until spring blossoms are ready again.

An alternative way of planting is to simply fill the box with potting soil over a layer of sand or gravel—to promote drainage—then set bedding plants into the soil. Seeds can be started indoors in winter and transplanted into the boxes in spring, or, if you're more patient than I, you can plant seeds directly in the boxes and wait for the plants to mature. If you choose to plant seeds you can start in late February or early March, depending on your climate, and use the box as a miniature greenhouse by covering it tightly with a plastic wrap or a plexiglass lid. This will raise the temperature of the soil and encourage early germination.

Another option is to simply purchase small bags of potting soil, puncture the bottoms to provide drainage, and insert bedding plants into slits cut into the top of the bag. The bags can be fitted easily into the boxes. As the seasons change, new plants in new bags can replace spent varieties. Don't waste the old soil, though; you can sprinkle it into the garden or use it in addition to organic matter to re-pot houseplants in the fall.

Window boxes will work in any location. Most annuals require bright, direct sun for a least four to six hours a day, but on the shady side of the house, elfin impatiens in a variety of colors will do just fine. Experiment with different locations: under a kitchen window, outside of the nursery, or beneath a sunny breakfast room window— wherever you place them, a box of brightly blooming flowers peeking in at you is a lovely and refreshing sight!

Deana Deck lives in Nashville, Tennessee, where her garden column is a regular feature in the Tennessean.

CRAFTWORKS

Cross Stitch Breadbasket Liner

Our breadbasket liner is simple to stitch and adds a colorful touch to a gift for any occasion. Follow the cross stitching instructions below for the liner, and then fill the basket with home-baked breads, muffins, cookies—whatever your own particular specialty. We've filled ours with a colorful tin full of tea, two beautiful china mugs, and some fresh baked muffins; but no matter what is inside, the message is the same: "A friend is what the heart needs all the time!"

Preparing the Fabric:

Model is worked on 14ct ivory aida. Cut fabric into 15" X 15" inch square. Ravel one half inch on edges and machine stitch to prevent further unravelling. Cross stitch fabric can also be purchased ready-made for breadbasket liners in craft stores.

Counted Cross Stitch:

Work one cross stitch to correspond to each coded square on chart. Stitches are worked as shown in Figure 1.

Backstitch:

For outline detail and lettering, backstitch as shown in Figure 2.

Figure 1

Figure 2

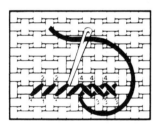

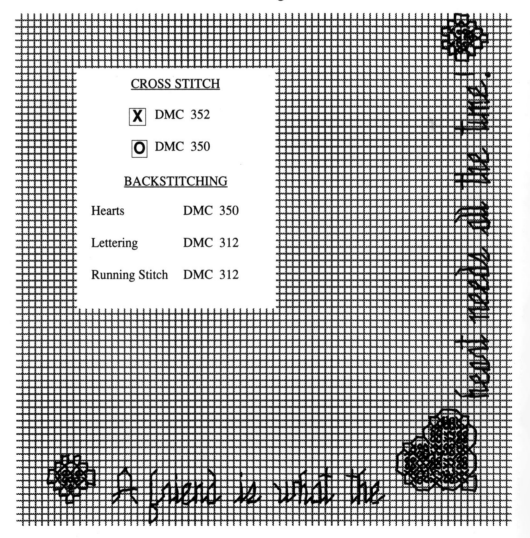

CROSS STITCH

| X | DMC 352 |
| O | DMC 350 |

BACKSTITCHING

Hearts	DMC 350
Lettering	DMC 312
Running Stitch	DMC 312

Precious Friend

Garnett Ann Schultz

God bless you, precious friend of mine
For all you've been to me,
For deep enrichment to my heart
And pleasures real I see,
There is no way that I could tell
The courage that you lend,
And yet somehow I still must say
I'm glad you are my friend.

God bless you for the tender faith
For every word you speak,
The comfort that you always bring—
So much I fondly seek.
Mere words alone can never tell
How quickly smiles are mine,
And I do hope you understand
You've made my days sublime.

You are the dearest joy on earth
The brightest hour of day,
The sun at dawn—the evening star
That lights a darkened way;
A shining dream—a glowing trust,
Your goodness knows no end,
That's why I tell you from my heart
God bless you, precious friend.

Intangible Friends

Reba L. Mitchell

No children rushing through the house
Demanding to be fed,
School halted fights and squabbles,
They grabbed their books and fled.
The house is heavenly quiet,
Some hours alone I spend,
To peacefully think and meditate,
Silence—you are my friend.

The days are so very busy,
Never a moment dull,
No time to waste on worry,
Because there is no lull.
You are my escape from tension,
Frazzled nerves you help me mend,
You drain all excess energy,
Work—you are my friend.

Little we learn as we go through life,
Experiences help us grow,
Sometimes lessons are painful
And often unbearably slow,
These golden years bring wisdom,
Most wrongs we learn to amend,
Our souls grow ripe and mellow,
Time—you are my friend.

TEATIME

Something sweet, something savory, and all delicious . . . this is the customary rule for foods served at tea. We offer you two different fresh-baked scones and a pumpkin date bread—three classic recipes to make your afternoon teatime a special time.

Lemon Blueberry Scones

3	cups buttermilk baking mix
4	tablespoons sugar
$1^1/2$	teaspoons grated lemon peel
1	cup fresh or frozen blueberries
3	eggs
$1/4$	cup milk

Preheat oven to 400°. In a medium bowl, combine baking mix, two tablespoons sugar, lemon peel, and blueberries. With fork, blend in two eggs beaten with milk. On lightly-floured baking sheet, press dough into circle 11 inches in diameter and $1/2$ inch thick. Brush with remaining egg, beaten, then sprinkle with remaining sugar. Cut into twelve wedges; separate wedges about $1/4$ inch apart. Bake twelve minutes or until golden. Serve hot with butter and preserves. Makes twelve scones.

English Scones

1	cup all-purpose flour
2	teaspoons baking powder
1	teaspoon sugar
$1/4$	teaspoon salt
3	tablespoons butter or margarine, softened
$1/4$	cup raisins or currants (optional)
5 to 6	tablespoons milk

Preheat oven to 450°. In a medium bowl, combine flour, baking powder, sugar, and salt. Cut in butter with pastry blender until mixture is the size of small peas.

Stir in raisins and enough milk to form a soft dough. On lightly-floured board, roll dough $1/2$ inch thick; cut into $1^1/2$-inch circles with round cookie cutter. Place on ungreased baking sheet and bake ten minutes or until golden. Serve warm with butter and assorted jams. Makes about twelve scones.

Pumpkin Date Bread

$3^1/2$	cups flour
3	cups sugar
$3/4$	teaspoon salt
2	teaspoons soda
$1^1/2$	teaspoons pumpkin pie spice
2	cups pumpkin
1	cup vegetable oil
4	eggs, beaten
$2/3$	cup water
1	cup walnuts, coarsely chopped
1	cup dates, chopped

Preheat oven to 350°. Combine the flour, sugar, salt, soda, and spice. Add the pumpkin, oil, eggs, and water. Mix until smooth. Stir in nuts and walnuts. Pour batter into three well-greased loaf pans. Bake 50 minutes or until bread tests done. Makes three loaves.

Bonnie Aeschliman is a teacher of occupational home economics and a freelance food consultant. She lives in Wichita, Kansas, with her husband and their two children.

Bits of Others

June Masters Bacher

We are shaped and we are fashioned
By the people that we know;
And from each we borrow something,
Taking it where we may go.

Often there is no returning,
For our journeys lead us on—
Lending to each new encounter
Bits of others we have known.

A Good Friend

Maxine Clark

A friend passed by and waved today,
And smiled as she drove her way.
I thought about her all day long—
Her buoyancy and cheerful song.
She left me with a joyful heart
And gave my day a grander start;
Though not a word was evidenced,
Her influence and radiance
Have buoyed me until day's end;
And I thank God for such a friend.

TRAVELER'S *Diary*

Marian H. Tidwell

East Family Dwelling, built in 1817.

Woman spinning in the shop run by the East Family sisters.

Shakertown at Pleasant Hill, Kentucky

As I turn into the drive that leads to Shakertown—the restored Shaker village at Pleasant Hill, Kentucky—a mist is slowly rising from the land as the sun continues its ascent in the east. The quiet of the morning, combined with the hand-stacked stone fences and acres of green fields that surround me, create an atmosphere decidedly detached from the modern world: immediately, Shakertown welcomes visitors into the nineteenth-century world of the American Shakers.

The village of Pleasant Hill was once the third largest settlement in the United States of the Shakers, a small, utopian religious group dedicated to the ideals of simplicity and utility and to the service of God. Shakers believe in communal living—males and females live as brother and sister in the Shaker community, not as husband and wife. Conversion and adoption are the Shaker means of continuity.

At Pleasant Hill visitors will find a near complete recreation of a nineteenth-century communal Shaker village. But this is more than a simple museum. Shakertown offers visitors the unique opportunity to learn about its people and their faith from the inside; guests are encouraged to stay in one of the seventy-two rooms scattered about the grounds, each furnished with exact replicas of Shaker furniture and other items from the Shakertown collections. This is not a static world of preserved artifacts and history, it is a living, functioning monument to one of our country's most fascinating religious groups.

My tour of Shakertown begins in the Centre Family Dwelling, where interpreters are on duty to lead visitors through the Shaker Life and Customs Exhibit, and to provide the basic historical background that will enlighten the remainder of their visit. The Centre Family Dwelling was once the place of honor in the community; Shakers divide themselves into families based on spiritual strength, and those living in the Centre Dwelling were leaders in the commune, their place of distinction marked by their Dwelling's proximity to the house of worship, called the Meeting House.

From the Centre Dwelling, it is a short walk to the East Family Dwelling, the center for Shakertown's craftspeople. Each morning, just as they did in the nineteenth century, craftspeople come to the East Family buildings for a full day of work. The women can be found in the East Family Sisters Shop, where they spin and weave and sew. The men work in the East Family Brethren Shop on broom making and cabinetry, and in the

Cooper's shop on buckets, churns, and cedar pails.

The craftspeople found at Shakertown today are employed by the village. Still, watching them, it is easy for me to imagine the peace that the Shakers found in this way of life. Their craftspeople worked long hours in these shops, motivated not by financial gain or the rewards of personal achievement, but by the Shaker belief that every task completed to the best of one's ability was a prayer to the Lord. Such selfless motivation created some of the most beautiful and lasting American furniture and architecture ever produced. Shakertown today offers demonstrations of these crafts, as well as the opportunity to purchase authentic handmade Shaker craft items.

Shakertown, located twenty-five miles southwest of Lexington, Kentucky, is open year round, except for Christmas Eve and Christmas Day. The village itself can be seen on one day's walking tour, but guests are encouraged to make their lodgings at Shakertown the center of a longer visit to Kentucky's surrounding bluegrass region. This is a wonderful idea. The atmosphere at Shakertown is quiet and peaceful and entirely conducive to the kind of relaxing vacation we all seek. And there is so much to see and learn. With lodgings located in the midst of the working village, the experience of Shakertown goes on beyond the original formal tour.

The Shakers are a truly fascinating group, one that seems less of an oddity the more one learns about its customs and beliefs. As you tour Shakertown, you will realize that evidence of the Shakers is everywhere in American life. They brought us the clothespin, the flat broom, the earliest washing machines, and countless other innovations in tools and craftsmanship. And while they have not flourished as a sect, the ideals that formed the foundation of their society are the very mainstream American ideals of equality —both of the sexes and of the races—conservation, utility, and self-sufficiency.

It was this self-sufficiency that the Board of Trustees at Shakertown worked so hard to reproduce in their living museum. When restoration began, they were meticulous about recreating every aspect of Shaker life; this goal proved to be true to another Shaker ideal—utilitarianism. With no large public grant money forthcoming, and no millionaire contributors, the village had to be self-sufficient in order to survive. And it is: today, Shakertown supports itself with money from admissions and from the sale of the crafts and other goods produced by its workers.

A trip to Shakertown is truly an enlightening experience. As I leave the grounds, I am enriched with a greater understanding of the Shaker people and their work, and a greater appreciation of the common values that held their community together. Even back in the modern world, a bit of the peace and the quiet of life I found at Shakertown remains with me.

Marian H. Tidwell is a freelance writer living in Johnson City, Tennessee.

Cooper at work in the village cooper shop.

29

Jane Addams

Nancy Skarmeas

I n 1889, Chicago's Nineteenth Ward was home to a diverse population of European immigrants. Russians, Greeks, Italians, Germans—they had all come to the United States looking for opportunity and freedom. What they found for the most part, however, was prejudice and isolation. As with nearly all immigrants in any time or place, language and cultural barriers put the Nineteenth Ward's residents at a disadvantage, and the barriers raised and bolstered by fear and prejudice kept them there.

Into this isolated world came Jane Addams, a young woman from an established American family, a woman with all the advantages these immigrants had hoped for when they set their sights on America. Well-educated, well-traveled, and well-off, Addams had no business moving into a neighborhood like the Nineteenth Ward. But move there she did; in 1889, she and a group of young women established Hull House—one of the United States' first settlement houses—and made it their home in the center of this inner city neighborhood.

The aim of a settlement house is to provide a

30

meeting place for the social workers who live there and the residents of the surrounding community, a place where the barriers of class, race, and nationality can be broken down. Addams and her staff welcomed the residents of the Ward into their home on an equal footing. They were to be neither clients nor subjects, but rather friends and neighbors.

Within a couple of years, Hull House had become the center of the community. Over forty clubs were organized there, as well as community day care, a gymnasium, sewing and cooking classes, language instruction, and more. And at the same time, Hull House workers led by Addams went to work using their own access to the channels of power to bring real change into the lives of their new neighbors. They lobbied for and achieved better factory working conditions, stricter child labor laws, and welfare reform; they gave a public voice to a community that had been entirely without, and they started the residents of the Nineteenth Ward on the road to assimilation into American life.

Hull House provided a model for social workers nationwide, and Jane Addams herself went on to a great career as an author and a speaker. During World War I she was active in the peace movement as a member of the Women's Peace Party and president of the International Congress of Women. She was awarded an honorary degree from Yale University, the first women to receive such recognition, and was also elected the first woman president of the National Conference of Charities and Correction. And through it all, she remained devoted to Hull House and active in its day-to-day operation. Today, social workers, sociologists, educators, and public officials draw upon her example for guidance in their own work, and much of what she achieved through Hull House is at the foundation of modern sociology.

What made her ideas so compelling and so powerful? Perhaps the fact that she was one of the first to approach America's growing immigrant population in the spirit of welcome rather than with closed-minded fear. She embraced the cultural diversity that these new Americans brought to the country, and she understood that what they needed was not isolation, nor was it condescending benevolence; what they needed was an equal opportunity to make lives for themselves in their new country.

Yet the most significant aspect of Jane Addams' philosophy is also the least considered. For while we admire her commitment and self-lessness, we are apt to ignore her own stated purpose. Time after time, in her writing, and the writings of those who knew her, appears Addams' insistence that the benefits of settlement work—of social work in general—belong as much to those doing the work as to those with whom they work. Jane Addams sincerely believed that she and the other members of society's privileged class gained wisdom and understanding through their exposure to members of a less fortunate class. And she believed that it was out of keeping with the Christian spirit to approach these people as saviors descending from above to lift them out of their oppression. To Addams, they were all members of the same community, and by helping any of them, she was helping all, including herself.

This is not to say that Jane Addams was a selfishly motivated person—no individual of such undying commitment can be considered so. But her philosophy does reveal an understanding of the need to break down the barriers that exist between people and between classes, not only so that those on the other side can become integrated, but so that one's own field of vision is expanded by the enlargement of the community.

The philosophy that drove Jane Addams to found Hull House and to devote her life's energies to its goals was perhaps inspired by her father, John Huy Addams, a leading abolitionist of his own day. From her father's example, Addams learned early the power inherent in her social position, and, more importantly, the responsibility for social action that must go along with that power.

Hull House, then, was not an isolated gesture of good will or a single act of charity. It was the realization of her basic belief that it is the responsibility of every member of society to break down the barriers that divide us and to work toward the integrated good of the whole.

How Lucky I Am

Garnett Ann Schultz

How lucky I am
How truly blessed too,
For I have a friend
And that friend is you.
I own the world
No question or doubt,
You are my gladness
All cares are left out.

How lucky I am
I know it is real,
Blue skies are smiling
Our joy is ideal,
Almost like springtime—
Joyous and bright,
Sun in the daytime;
Starshine at night.

Dreams are abundant
Laughter is mine,
Everything lovely,
Precious, and fine.
My heart walks on cloudsteps
Within a blue sky.
A new day is dawning,
How lucky am I.

Photo Opposite
Robert Wagoner/The Stock Market

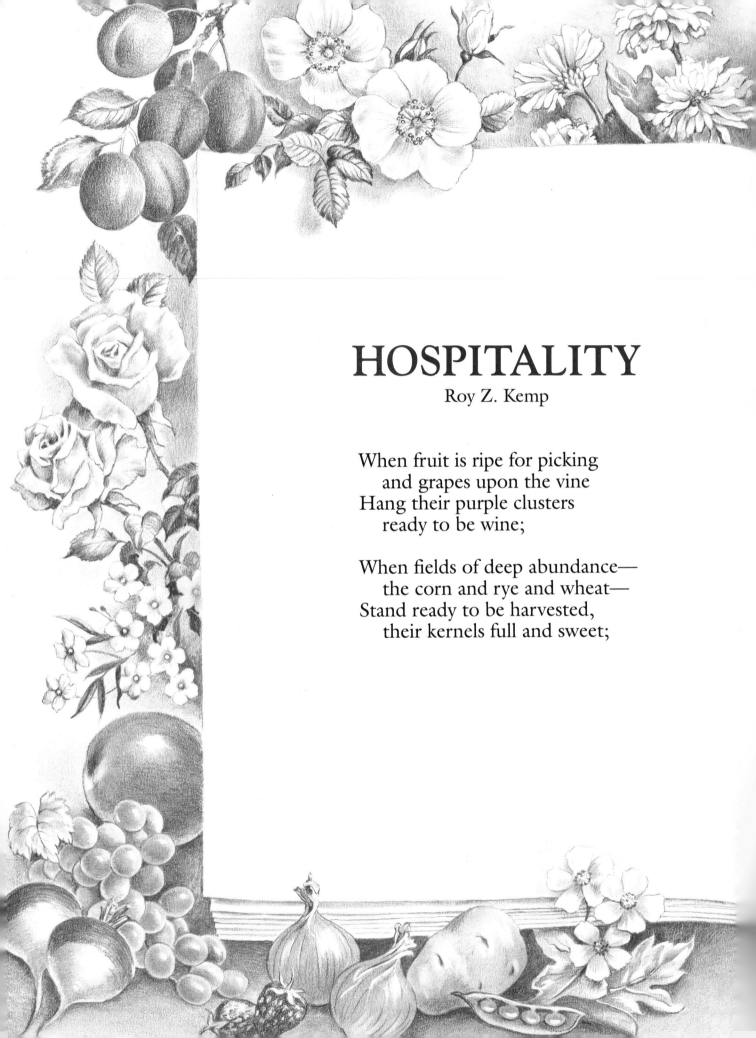

HOSPITALITY

Roy Z. Kemp

When fruit is ripe for picking
   and grapes upon the vine
Hang their purple clusters
   ready to be wine;

When fields of deep abundance—
   the corn and rye and wheat—
Stand ready to be harvested,
   their kernels full and sweet;

When gardens overflow
   with vegetables and greens:
Tomatoes, squash, and carrots,
   potatoes, lettuce, beans;

May there be those beside me
   who hunger to be fed!
I could not take this feast alone,
   I could not break my bread,

But with someone to share my food,
   to share the harvesttime—
The food and drink are precious things—
   companionship divine!

COLLECTOR'S CORNER

Family Trees

Hunting for your ancestors can be one of the most satisfying forms of collecting. Instead of porcelain or antique books, you are gathering the puzzle pieces of your own history. With the increased mobility of our society, many of us have lost the connection between ourselves and the generations before us. By learning about our ancestors, we begin the process of bridging the gap between past and present.

Although they're similar, family trees and family histories are not the same. A family tree is a listing of the genealogical, or lineal, descent of a family—just the facts. The family history adds substance to the family tree by weaving in details of background, and experiences, and personalities. This is the place for intriguing stories and tidbits of information; like the teacake recipe that Great Grandmother Baird always used at Christmas or Granddaddy Pierce's experiences as an Army cook in World War I.

The task of tracing your family's ancestors might seem monumental at first. However, when taken one step at a time, it can be a fulfilling and exciting pursuit.

The search begins with yourself and your immediate family. By beginning in the present and gradually stepping back into the past, you assure that you don't waste time on false leads; remember, the fact that an historical figure had the same surname as your family does not guarantee that you are related. Thus, when looking for information, begin with the people you know—your parents, grandparents, great-grandparents, aunts, uncles, and cousins—the information you gather from these living people will provide a solid foundation for a search further into your family's past.

A three-ring binder is helpful for keeping your information organized. Write the full name of each relative you know at the top of a sheet of paper—one name per sheet—and then write down all that you know about each person, beginning with date of birth, marriage, and death. This is a good preparation for your search and will ensure that valuable information is not lost or misplaced. As your search progresses, remember to take into consideration all the possible variations of your name: Smith, Smythe, Smithe, Schmitt, etc. Although your name might have been consistent for the past couple of generations, your not-so-distant ancestors might very well have spelled it differently.

If you have older living relatives, call or visit and ask questions. Your purpose is to add names and verification to your family tree, and details and stories to your family history. Although paper and pencil are the only necessary materials, a tape recorder or video recorder frees you to listen without the worry of missing some important piece of news while intent upon writing.

Once you have exhausted your living relatives, a good source for additional genealogical information is the National Archives in Washington, D.C., where you can find public and legal documents of all kinds, from war records from the American wars before World War II to deeds and wills and records of immigration and naturalization. There are also eleven regional branches of the Archives located throughout the country, and if you cannot actually visit, the Archives will answer written requests for information and research.

Many people are not aware that all public records are just that—public. Access to birth and death certificates, deeds, wills, war records, and much more is open to all Americans, and copies of these records can be made for a very small fee. Your state's Archives, Department of Health, and Register of Deeds are all possible sources of such records. And if you are looking for a particular bit of information and do not know just where to go, call the information number for your state capital; they will be able to give you the name and number of the office you need. Of course, don't forget to take advantage of information available in local libraries and book stores, and to visit the local historical society. They, too, will have valuable records, and may also be able to give you some guidance in your search.

Cemeteries also contain a wealth of information. In addition to birth and death dates, you can frequently find epitaphs that add spice and texture to your family history. To keep headstone information for future reference, photograph it,

or use a large sheet of paper and a crayon to make a rubbing. Make sure to check with the people in charge of the particular cemetery before you make a rubbing; some cemeteries limit rubbings in order to preserve older headstones.

The key to researching your family tree is to be persistent and creative; in addition to public records and official documents, don't forget family Bibles, baby books, boxes of clippings, diaries, scrapbooks, and old photographs. And don't be disappointed to find gaps in your family tree. If you traced your forebearers back to the early 1600s, you would find over sixteen thousand people directly related to you, and that's not counting siblings! With that number of ancestors, it's no wonder that some are difficult or impossible to locate.

The jigsaw puzzle of your family tree will never be complete, but each time you find another piece, you gain further understanding and insight into the people and events that made you who you are. Building a family tree, like building a family, is an ongoing project, one that is always growing and expanding, and always offering new rewards for the hard work put in.

Carol Shaw Johnston, a public school teacher, writes articles and short stories. She lives with her family in Brentwood, Tennessee.

THROUGH MY WINDOW

Pamela Kennedy

Friends

A while back, a friend of mine was working on her dissertation for a Ph.D. in Sociology. Her paper had to do with interpersonal relationships among women. Basi-cally, it was about friendships and how we make them, define them, and maintain them. My friend passed out questionnaires in our neighborhood and we all filled them out and did lots of thinking

38

about friends. I found myself pondering friends and friendships long after I had given back the questionnaire and I'm eager to see the results because I'm not too sure I ever did figure out what makes someone a friend.

One day, however, I heard my son mention that a formerly inseparable companion and he were no longer friends. "How do you know?" I inquired. He looked at me with that look reserved for parents and little sisters, incredulous that anyone could even ask such a ridiculous question.

"You just know, Mom. Everybody knows that kind of stuff."

"Everybody" usually means everybody in his particular sphere of existence, so I decided to tap into this wellspring of ten-year-old understanding. Next day I polled seventy-five local fourth and fifth graders, asking each to define "best friend." My son was right. Everybody knew. There wasn't one blank paper. And just in case you've forgotten what everyone knows at age ten, I'd like to share some of these valuable insights.

Secrets are a big factor in friendships. Best friends have secrets, but always share them with each other. They never, never tell them to anyone else, however. I guess that gets a bit tricky if you stop being best friends with someone and have already shared your entire cache of secrets —maybe you need to make up new ones to share with your current friend.

The secrets you share have to be true though, because most of the kids agreed that best friends never lie. They also never cheat, take your stuff, hit you, or use bad words.

Aside from being moral paragons, best friends listen to your problems, are there when you need them, and sit with you when you're sad. I could add a hearty "Amen" here. There's nothing like having a friend sit with you when you're sad.

And friends never hurt your feelings, call you names, or ignore you either. When you are down, a best friend believes in you and sticks up for you—but is never stuck up and would never put you down.

It reassured me to know that best friends don't care about how you look, if you have "expansive" (I'm sure she meant *expensive*) jeans or if your hair grows right! That last one certainly eased my mind!

Ten-year-olds don't just generalize about friendships either, they get into the real nuts and bolts of the subject. For one thing, best friends don't ever trip you in the hall. Now, anyone could see where that would put a real dent in a friendship.

Best friends always ask you to spend the night over at their houses and their Moms never say "No." They never like who you like, or tell who you like, especially to the person you really like. (Think like a ten-year-old victim of unrequited love to figure out that one.)

When you spend the night with your best friend—whose mother never says "No"—you should always have a pillow fight. While there, your best friend should never hog the video games or eat stuff in front of you or tell you to shut up and go to sleep! And if you tell someone he or she is your best friend, you'd better not let them hear you saying the same thing to someone else!

Although the qualities of mercy and understanding seem highly valued by these friend-experts, I found one young lady's comments most revealing: "A best friend should be nice and share, should not be mean and fight, and you should never give that person more than two chances."

I think it would be a wonderful world if we could all have best friends who were giving and kind, who shared some delicious secrets and invited us over for pillow fights. And we certainly could all benefit from having a friend who would sit beside us when we are sad and who wouldn't care about our jeans. But I think those of us who have lived well beyond the age of ten would have to take issue with at least two points: There are times when everyone needs to shut up and go to sleep and we all need way more than two chances!

Pamela Kennedy is a freelance writer of short stories, articles, essays, and children's books. Married to a naval officer and mother of three children, she has made her home on both U.S. coasts and currently resides in Hawaii. She draws her material from her own experiences and memories, adding bits of imagination to create a story or mood.

Child's Play

My Bed Is a Boat

Robert Louis Stevenson

My bed is like a little boat;
  Nurse helps me in when I embark;
She girds me in my sailor's coat,
  And starts me in the dark.

At night, I go on board and say
  Good night to all my friends on shore;
I shut my eyes and sail away
  And see and hear no more.

And sometimes things to bed I take,
  As prudent sailors have to do;
Perhaps a slice of wedding cake,
  Perhaps a toy or two.

All night across the dark we steer;
  But when the day returns at last,
Safe in my room, beside the pier,
  I find my vessel fast.

50 YEARS AGO

British girls prepare Christmas cards for mailing home to England from their temporary schools in the U.S.   Photo courtesy of UPI/Bettmann

New School Ties

Limey!" hooted toughies. "I say, ole chap," they drawled, making monocles with their fingers. With such normal antics pupils in many a U.S. school this month greeted their small British guests. But by last week most of Britain's 2,700 young evacuees in the U.S. had begun to feel at home in U.S. schools. Teachers and pupils chuckled over differences in U.S. and British education.

Because they had attended prep or "public" (British for private) schools in England, most of the 2,700 were placed in U.S. private schools.

Little Britons were surprised to find that most U.S. pupils wear no school uniforms. Skinnier than their U.S. contemporaries, they found the food much better than in British schools, quickly put on weight. They missed tea, got used to drinking milk instead, were delighted with unaccustomed shower baths and pencil sharpeners.

British boys found classes more informal and discipline less strict in U.S. schools, were shocked to discover that U.S. pupils are never caned. They startled strangers by tipping their hats, surprised their classmates by jumping to their feet whenever a teacher entered their classroom. In classes, British pupils showed they knew more of world affairs (more even than some of their teachers), were far ahead of their classmates in vocabulary and foreign languages, not so good in mathematics and spelling, pretty bad in Western Hemisphere geography and U.S. history. On one thing they agreed: they had to study harder in Britain. Said one of them: "In our country, they give you more than you can do in the way of studies, and then do not expect you to do it all. Here they give you just enough, and expect you to do it."

HAPPY GIRLS

Caroline Eyring Miner

Happy girls, I envy you,
Fresh as roses kissed with dew,
Fragrant as their perfume rare
Scattered freely everywhere.

On tiptoe you greet the dawn
Dancing over emerald lawn;
Eager for the day to start,
Facing life with laughing heart.

Shining stars are in your eyes,
Jeweled dreams from sunny skies,
Dreams about another day
When True Love will come to stay.

Beautiful you are, as mist,
Rainbow-hued, and gently kissed,
Dressed so daintily and trim,
Lithe as willows, and as slim.

Happy girls, I envy you
Your tomorrows bright and new.
Keep your eager, happy ways
To make joyous future days.

— Edgar A. Guest —

Little Boy Dressing

Wonder what he dreams about,
    Little wide-eyed drowsy head,
Through the window staring out,
    Sitting, cross-legged, on the bed?
Stocking only halfway on,
    Like a statue cut in stone,
Time for dressing almost gone;
    Lost, he seems, in fancy's zone.

Half an hour ago we said:
    "Hurry! you'll be late for school!
Hurry! tumble out of bed!
    Hurry! that's the morning rule!"
Still his clothes are on the chair.
    Still he sits and looks afar.
Wonder, as we watch him there,
    What his thoughts and visions are.

Don't remember as a lad,
    When I dawdled as does he,
Just what thoughts and dreams I had
    And what fancies came to me.
All I know is that I sat,
    As did Mother Goose's John,
Staring at the world like that—
    Stocking halfway off and on.

Edgar A. Guest began his illustrious career in 1895 at the age of fourteen when his work appeared in the Detroit Free Press. *His column was syndicated in over 300 newspapers, and he became known as ''The Poet of the People.'' Mr. Guest captured the hearts of vast radio audiences with his weekly program, ''It Can Be Done'' and, until his death in 1959, published many treasured volumes of poetry.*

Heart's Desire

Hilda Butler Farr

I'd like to gather all my friends
Beneath our roof some day,
The ones whose years are only few—
And those with hair of gray.
I'd bring them from across the seas
From mountains, hills, and vales,
And those who travel constantly
Could spin their many tales.
Musicians who could sing for us
The old and modern themes,
Artistic friends whose brushes paint
The pictures of our dreams.
The ones who have no thought of wealth
Whose hearts are purest gold,
And those who've found the loneliness
Success can sometimes hold.
Each one has touched my life with joy
Somewhere along the way—
I'd like to gather all of them
Beneath our roof some day.

Photo Opposite
Wiscasset, Maine
Fred Sieb Photograph

BITS & PIECES

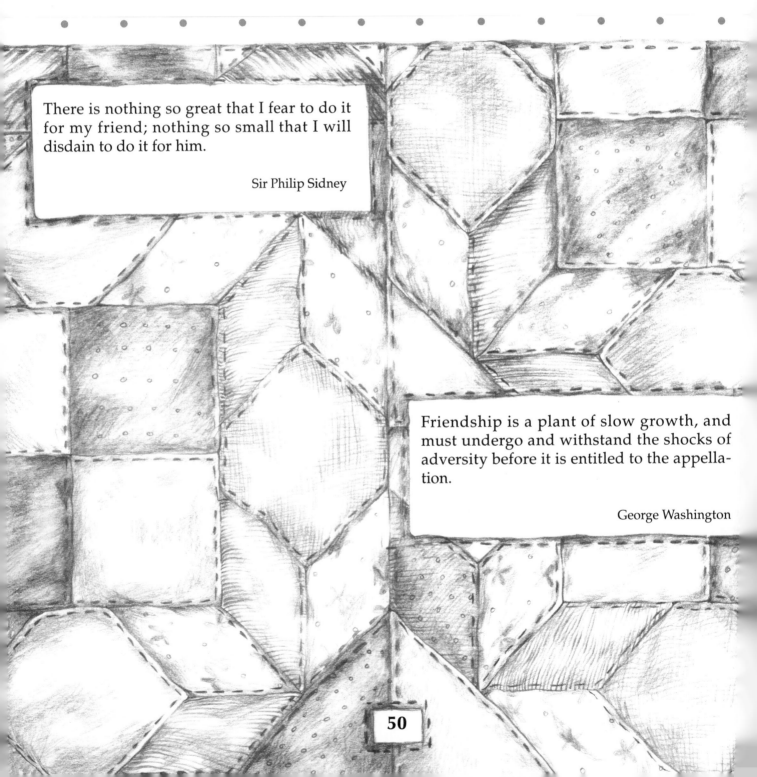

There is nothing so great that I fear to do it for my friend; nothing so small that I will disdain to do it for him.

Sir Philip Sidney

Friendship is a plant of slow growth, and must undergo and withstand the shocks of adversity before it is entitled to the appellation.

George Washington

The only way to have a friend is to be one.

Ralph Waldo Emerson

Friendship improves happiness, and abates misery, by doubling our joy, and dividing our grief.

Joseph Addison

A true friend is a gift of God, and He only who made hearts can unite them.

Robert South

If a man does not make new acquaintances as he passes through life, he will soon find himself left alone. A man should keep his friendships in constant repair.

Samuel Johnson

The Family Within

Maxine Hartley

Welcome to my home:
Come inside—there's friendship here,
Laughter you are sure to hear,
Happiness is yours to share
With people who sincerely care.

This is my home:
The stately rooms, so neatly kept,
The bed upstairs in which I've slept,
The people here, so good and true
With smiles of warmth to welcome you.

These are my people:
I'll not forget those memories
I've shared here, with my family,
Memories both good and bad.
Loving care I've always had.

This is your home:
You've found a haven from unrest;
Come inside—find happiness.
All who enter through this door
Are friends of ours for evermore.

Jessie Walker, Photographer

HAPPINESS

Betty Baldwin

Happiness is not dependent upon material possessions." We've all heard that admonition, and it sounds great, but life just wouldn't be the same without some of our favorite things, possessions that have little to do with monetary value or practicality, but add greatly to the quality of our lives.

A china pin tray with a fox perched on the rim that was always a part of my mother's dressing table now holds pins on my bathroom counter. One side is faintly smudged by a fire that destroyed our house but left this one small bit of china intact.

Afghans that add a splash of color spark memories of my mother expertly plying her crochet hook as she talked with visitors or watched TV. Dad's old footstool is a little shabby, but it has withstood the onslaught of more than a dozen grandchildren tumbling about at his feet as he sat in his favorite chair.

Two hand-painted china baby cups, one with a chipped rim, were used first by my husband's father and mother and now occupy a

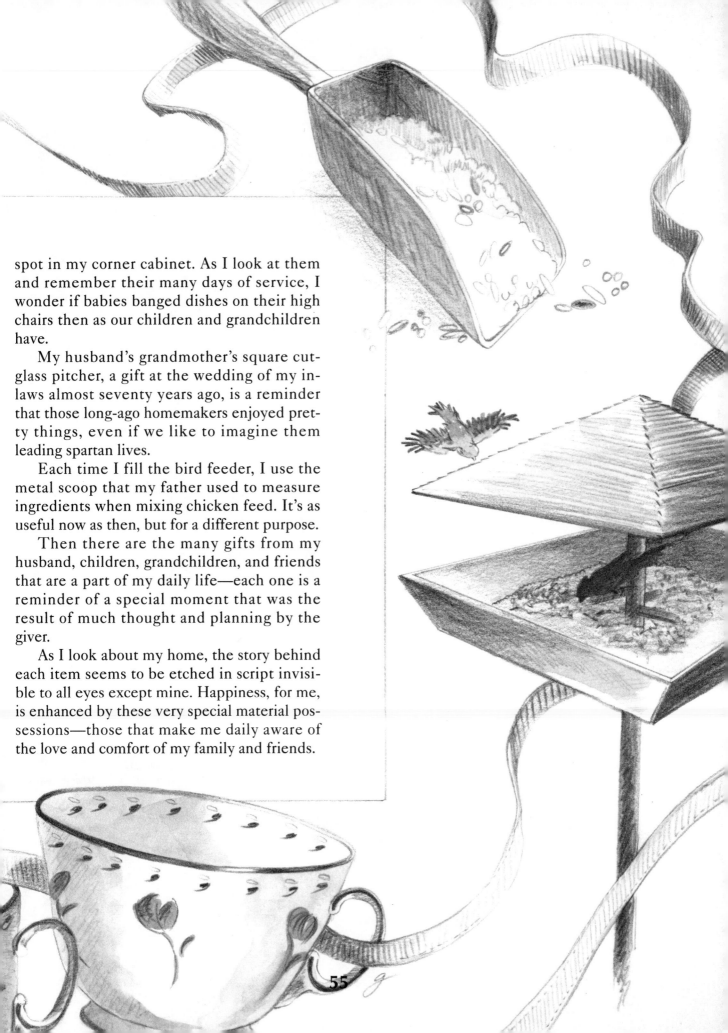

spot in my corner cabinet. As I look at them and remember their many days of service, I wonder if babies banged dishes on their high chairs then as our children and grandchildren have.

My husband's grandmother's square cut-glass pitcher, a gift at the wedding of my in-laws almost seventy years ago, is a reminder that those long-ago homemakers enjoyed pretty things, even if we like to imagine them leading spartan lives.

Each time I fill the bird feeder, I use the metal scoop that my father used to measure ingredients when mixing chicken feed. It's as useful now as then, but for a different purpose.

Then there are the many gifts from my husband, children, grandchildren, and friends that are a part of my daily life—each one is a reminder of a special moment that was the result of much thought and planning by the giver.

As I look about my home, the story behind each item seems to be etched in script invisible to all eyes except mine. Happiness, for me, is enhanced by these very special material possessions—those that make me daily aware of the love and comfort of my family and friends.

INTERIOR DECORATING

Eunice Mackinson

I'm covering my cushions
   with hues and tints of Fall:
Russet, orange, yellow, brown;
   my house will hold them all.

I'll put some flowers in a vase
   to brighten up the room;
Fall's many varied colors
   will chase away the gloom

Of summer's final passing,
   and as I start each day,
My spirits will be lifted
   by Autumn's bright array.

Antiques and Flowers
North Conway, New Hampshire
Fred Sieb Photography

Country
CHRONICLE
Lansing Christman

Meadowdale. There is music in the name, music of the sweetest kind, flowing with the voices and the sounds of the land. Meadowdale was a farming area of flatlands where workers of the soil were neighbors and friends. Together they went to church and attended community events and social affairs; they built friendships that endured.

Today Meadowdale has yielded to urban sprawl; houses have replaced growing crops and grazing cows in these wide-stretching flats between the Helderberg Mountains and the city of Albany, New York.

There is little left of the Meadowdale I knew as a boy, when I would travel there by horse and wagon with my father and mother to visit friends. In later years, I went there often in all seasons of the year. I went in spring during planting, and again in summer when crops were ripening. I went in September when sumac leaves along the

58

roadsides were red as embers in a hearth and the maples were crowned in reds and golds.

Perhaps only Meadowdale Road identifies the place today. The one-room schoolhouse is gone. So is the old depot by the tracks. No passenger trains use the line, but the freights still run.

There was a time when Meadowdale's name matched its bucolic setting. There were meadows of hay, fields of grain, pastures, woodlots, and gentle streams. There were gardens, orchards, and vineyards. Sometimes I wish I were a poet, so that I could write an ode to Meadowdale filled with the pastoral beauty that I knew. Or I wish I were a composer, perhaps. Then I would produce a symphony as charming and enchanting as DeBussy's "Afternoon of a Faun," a flowing symphony with the rhythm and music of the meadows and dales that I loved.

Few remember the old Meadowdale, and though I do, still, I do not wish to go back. The memories tucked away in the corner of my heart keep Meadowdale a sanctuary where men of the land worked and lived, a place where they found enduring friendships and content.

_____

The author of two published books, Lansing Christman has been contributing to Ideals *for almost twenty years. Mr. Christman has also been published in several American, foreign, and braille anthologies. He lives in rural South Carolina.*

Photo Overleaf
Qu'Appelle Valley
Saskatchewan, Canada
George Hunter/H. Armstrong Roberts, Inc.

Letter of
My Thoughts

Craig E. Sathoff

I've written you in thoughts, my friend,
So often through the years,
But somehow ink just couldn't find
The words to make thoughts clear.

Within my thoughts I have relived
Those happy times we shared
As childhood friends who ran and played
Without the slightest care.

You were a friend to me back then,
And still you are today,
For memories can give us strength
And help us on our way.

In my thoughts I've thanked you, friend,
Though surely not enough,
For your example years ago
Still helps when times are rough.

I've often written in my thoughts,
But here at last are words
To say I thank you for the joys
That in my heart you've stirred.

ST. MATTHEWS
✝ CHURCH ✝
EPISCOPAL

SUNDAY SERVICES
· AT ·
10 A.M.

DURING
JULY and AUGUST
and
ONE SUNDAY IN SEPTEMBER

To a Shut-In

Betty W. Stoffel

Forgive us if we seem to be
So wrapped in living selfishly;
It must be hard behind a wall
To look for friends who never call;
For those of us with jobs to do
Forget there are no jobs for you,
And we who move with busy feet
Forget you never walk a street;
And so we tread our daily groove
Forgetting that you cannot move,
Till in the maze of much to do
We spend the time we saved for you.
Forgive us friend, be patient, kind,
Your feet are lame, but we are blind;
What good are eyes that fail to see
Another's need for sympathy?
What good are feet that never boast
Of going where they're needed most?
Or fail to make a life more sweet?
I think we're blind, though we have feet.

My Thanks for Others
Margaret Rorke

O Lord, how very much I owe
To others whom You've let me know
   And see from day to day—
The young, the old, the in-between
Who make an entrance in the scene
   In which I'm called to play.

Another's sweet, approving smile
Can make my efforts seem worthwhile
   And crown my will to try.
Encouragement another speaks
Is oft the spur my spirit seeks
   Though not quite knowing why.

And, yes, I'm grateful too
For those who have a dimmer view
   Of me and my poor part
Because they challenge me to test
What's truly noble, pure, and best
   Within my mind and heart.

I often wonder how I'd be
Without the folks surrounding me—
   My vital, living hem.
That's why I pause to give this prayer
To You it pleased to put them there.
   I thank you, Lord, for them.

For
Mommie

National Symphony
presents
Mozart

My Heart Is Knowing

Georgia Moore Eberling

The first gold leaf dropped down today;
The butterflies are still at play
In a white and yellow cloud, that's way
Above the lawn, the bees still stray
Among the flowers. Not far away
The autumn walks, for just today
The first gold leaf fell down.

I shall not grieve for summer's going,
Today the sweet south wind is blowing,
And high above white clouds are glowing
In September haze, while vines are showing
A tinge of red. My heart is knowing
That autumn comes . . . there is no slowing
The pace of Time . . . but autumn brings
The harvest, and glad strength for wings.

Autumn Memories

Blythe G. Sears

Of Autumn scenes, I best remember these:
The touch of gold gilding grass and trees.
The scent of fresh mown hay and garnered grain,
The smoke of burning leaves in country lanes;
A flash of scarlet in a grosbeak's coat,
A spray of song flung from its tiny throat;
Rugose persimmons, ripening, abound
While chinquapins and chestnuts pelt the ground.
In gardens, marigolds and asters nod
And roads are edged with plumes of goldenrod.
The artist Nature waits with lighted fuse
To set the woods afire in flaming hues;

Blue lakes where age-bent willows stoop to drink,
The purple haze when day begins to sink.
The dimuendo of the insect choir
Reveals a message—they will soon retire;
Dim roads where moonlight casts an eerie spell,
Winrows of hay running parallel;
Wild geese, in V-formation flying high—
We love to hear them honk as they go by.
Beside the road a solitary birch;
On withered limbs, an owl finds a perch;
The tinted leaves adrift on languid streams
Are painted boats transporting summer's dreams.

Seasonal Change

Goldenrod and milkweed pods,
Purple asters bending,
Ripe red apples hanging low
Tell of summer's ending.
Withered vines, brown curled leaves,
Morning air grows cool,
Children wait in happy groups
The bus they ride to school.
Farewell dear summer, it is time
For you to slip away,
And in your place with frosted lace,
A welcomed autumn day.

Rita Fay Farnham
DeSoto, Missouri

Indian Summer

Squash colored leaves
Litter the trails of ransacking squirrels
While sleepy scarecrows in patchwork rags
Mottle the countryside,
Their scraggly straw arms
Dangling in the balmy breeze
Of Indian summer.
And the geese in a thousand Vs
Come honking overhead
Riding the last brilliant breath
Of September.

Kathleen M. Rodgers
Alexandria, Louisiana

Editor's Note: Readers are invited to submit unpublished, original poetry, short anecdotes, and humorous reflections on life for possible publication in future *Ideals* issues. Please send copies only; manuscripts will not be returned. Writers receive $10 for each published submission. Send material to "Readers' Reflections," Ideals Publishing Corporation, P.O. Box 140300, Nashville, Tennessee, 37214-0300.

Reflections

October

October's hair is golden,
Her eyes are Heaven's blue,
Her lips are magic sweetness—
The mist of Autumn dew.

Like red-ripe luscious berries
Nestling on a vine,
I am October's lover,
I claim her kisses mine.

Her gown is all embroidered
With rich grape applique
And bows of brightest sumac red
Enhance her manner gay.

Lightest of caresses
Her jeweled fingertips bestow
Until the morning air
Becomes a luminescent glow.

And I drink its dewey freshness
All about my face,
And sniff sweet cider fragrance
From some orchard valley place.

While out walking in October,
My feet are wont to stray
Back to a lovely garden wall
Where friendly asters sway.

A bank of white chrysanthemums
See us go by and nod,
For October is the princess
Crowned by the graciousness of God!

Bernice Crawford
Independence, Missouri

73

Old Friends

Linnea Holmberg Bodman

How nice it is to visit friends
    You haven't seen for years.
They don't look quite the same, and yet
    Old friendship reappears.

There's first the shock of seeing that
    They've aged much more than you—
And then the quick suspicion that
    You've been aging too!

You sit and talk about the past
    And laugh at old time jokes,
And find out what has happened to
    Some long "lost-track-of" folks.

And very soon the years between
    Just seem to disappear,
And all of you are young and gay
    As in that yesteryear.

Yes, it is nice to visit friends—
    Old friends—those that last.
They bring a joy that only comes
    With friends out of your past.

Reunion

Julie Beall Jett

I'm glad we met today, my friend,
    To take some time to share,
We laughed and talked and shed some tears
    And laid aside our cares.

We wandered back to yesterday,
    A younger you and me—
Remembering when hopes were high
    And dreams were had for free.

We dusted off old memories,
    The happy and the sad:
The things we did, the way we were,
    And all the joy we had.

You took my hand, and walking back
    We stopped along the way
To look along the paths we took
    That led us to today.

So promise that we'll meet again,
    This day has meant so much
Unknown tomorrows lie ahead,
    But friends must keep in touch!

75

Photo Overleaf
Near East Orange, Vermont
Dianne Dietrich Leis Photo

Return of Autumn

Betty A. Collier

Orion rises o'er the dunes;
The crickets fiddle tiny tunes;
A sapphire sea, an opal sky
Invite the soul, delight the eye.

Velvety plumes of goldenrod
And starry purple asters nod;
With streaming manes of rainbow spray,
The breakers leap as to the fray.

Each hour flows like a peaceful stream,
A fragment of a happy dream:
To spend in winter's dismal cold
We hoard September's lavish gold.

September

Rose Koralewsky

Disheveled clouds,
  untidying the sky,
Hurled here and there
  by fitful gusts of wind,
Swiftly draw thick veils
  across the eye
Of heaven, where the stars
  have come unpinned.

Crisped shreds of leaves
  are winrowed in the lane;
The birds are mute,
  lined up along the wires;
And recognizing Autumn's
  old refrain,
I go inside to start
  the winter fires.

Readers' Forum

Your magazine represents a great American panacea! Whenever I am disenchanted about life, my cure is to pick up the latest edition of Ideals, *and existence beams once more. I am a seventh-grade language arts teacher and read often to my students gems found in* Ideals. *My kids simply revere it. . . May God continue to bless you, your staff, and of course that MASTERPIECE* Ideals!

Doris A. Ezell
Rock Hill, South Carolina

Ideals *is indeed a breath of fresh air. It deals with the beauties around us, and it is a real pleasure . . . I hope to never be without it.*

Marion Gillespie
Brooklyn, Michigan

I would just like to thank you so much for the prompt and efficient manner in which you handled my gift subscription to Ideals, *myself being the recipient of the gift. . . . It has been so nice to leisurely peruse these issues at this quiet time of the year and has brought immense joy to my husband and myself. Thank you again for caring to keep your customers satisfied.*

Mrs. Edward L. Sneed
Warwick, Rhode Island

Ed: In our 1990 Easter issue, we neglected to give credit for the photos in our Traveler's Diary feature, "Honolulu's Iolani Palace." The color photos on pages 68 and 69 of the article are courtesy of The Friends of Iolani Palace; the two sepia images on the following spread were provided by the Hawaii State Archives. We apologize to both organizations.

Remember your friends with a copy of FRIENDSHIP IDEALS.

Order now and receive 5 copies of *Friendship Ideals.* Each comes with its own large greeting envelope to make the gift special. Only $16.95, plus $2.00 postage and handling.

Order # IO7642A

Need a hostess gift? Ideals cookbooks make an excellent yet inexpensive way to say "Thank you." Retailing for $3.95 each book, these cookbooks are now available for only $9.95 plus $2.00 postage and handling for a set of three.

Set #1: *Guide to Microwave Cooking, 30-Minute Meals, Casseroles and One-Dish Meals.*

Order # IO7639A

Set #2: *Low Calorie, Light Menus, Light and Delicious* (a sugar-free title). Order # IO7638A

Send check or money order to:

Ideals Friendship
P.O. Box 148000
Nashville, TN 37214-8000

Or call TOLL-FREE 1-800-558-4343
to order by credit card.

Celebrating Life's Most Treasured Moments